SHRED IT!

RIPPIN' AND RIDIN' EXTREME SNOWBOARDING

Virginia Loh-Hagan

45TH PARALLEL PRESS

Ann Arbor, Michigan

www.cherrylakepublishing.com

Content Adviser: Liv Williams, Editor, iLivExtreme

Reading Adviser: Beth Walker Gambro, MS, Ed., Reading Consultant, Yorkville, IL

Photo Credits: © Artur Didyk/Shutterstock, cover, title page; © Austin Colbert/The Aspen Times via AP, File, 5; © Aflo Co. Ltd./Alamy , 6; Oleg Yunakov / CC BY-SA 4.0, CC BY-SA 4.0 via Wikimedia Commons, 7; © Chad Chomlack/Red Bull Content Pool, 8; © Daniel Milchev/Red Bull Content Pool, 9; Invented by Sherman R. Poppen, assigned to Brunswick Corporation uploaded by User:Lar, Public domain, via Wikimedia Commons, 11; © Dmitry Molchanov/Shutterstock, 12; © Kofimage/Shutterstock, 15; © localcinema/Shutterstock,16–17; © LiveMedia/Shutterstock, 18–19; © Maxim Petrichuk/Shutterstock, 20–21; © Media Drum World/Alamy, 22; © Tomas Marek/Shutterstock, 25, © Goinyk Production/Shutterstock, 26; © dpa picture alliance/Alamy, 28

Library of Congress Cataloging-in-Publication Data has been filed and is available at catalog.loc.gov

Cherry Lake Press would like to acknowledge the work of the Partnership for 21st Century Learning, a Network of Battelle for Kids. Please visit Battelle for Kids online for more information.

Printed in the United States of America

Note from publisher: Websites change regularly, and their future contents are outside of our control. Supervise children when conducting any recommended online searches for extended learning opportunities.

ABOUT THE AUTHOR

Virginia Loh-Hagan is an author, university professor, former classroom teacher, and curriculum designer. In college, she jumped off a bunk bed and broke her toe. No more jumping for her. She lives in San Diego with her very tall husband and very naughty dogs.

Table of Contents

CHAPTER 1

No Limits!

Extreme snowboarders **shred** no matter what. Shredding means riding hard and fast.

In 2023, Gaon Choi rocked the **halfpipe** event. The halfpipe is a U-shaped ramp. Choi soared up the ramp. She spun. She grabbed the board. She kept spinning. She landed. And then she did it again and again.

Gaon Choi competing in the X Games snowboarding halfpipe final in 2023.

Chloe Kim won 2 gold medals in the 2022 Olympics. She won her third halfpipe world championship in March 2025.

And she won! Choi got a gold medal. She became the youngest halfpipe snowboarding champ at the X Games. Choi took the record from Chloe Kim. Kim is a snowboarding legend. Kim helped train Choi.

SHRED IT! SPOTLIGHT:

Amy Purdy

Amy Purdy is a double amputee. At 19, she lost both her legs below the knee. She learned to accept her reality. But she didn't accept limitations. She built her own **prosthetic** legs. Prosthetic describes an artificial limb. She was snowboarding 7 months later. Purdy said, "My legs haven't disabled me, if anything they've enabled me. They've forced me to rely on my imagination and to believe in the possibilities, and that's why I believe that our imaginations can be used as tools for breaking through borders, because in our minds, we can do anything and we can be anything." Watch Amy Purdy's TED Talk titled "Living Beyond Limits."

AMY PURDY, 2024

Extreme snowboarders ride the steepest slopes. They **rip** the deepest snow. Rip means to cut through. They get the biggest air. Choi and Kim didn't let their age stop them. And snowboarders don't let other challenges get in their way.

That's the spirit of extreme snowboarding. Riders don't see limitations. They see opportunities to do the impossible.

Travis Rice is one of the greatest extreme snowboarders. He jumped a 120-foot (36.5-m) gap in Utah. He was the first to land a 1080. This is 3 full spins in the air. He said, "Adventure is what you make of it."

Shaun White retired from competitive snowboarding after the 2022 Olympic Games. He holds the world record for most X Games and Olympic Games gold medals for snowboarding.

Tom Sims and Jake Burton Carpenter were inspired by Poppen. They were **rivals**. Rivals compete against each other. They wanted to be the best. They kept making snowboards better. They added **bindings**. Bindings are straps that hold the boots in place. This makes boards easier to control.

These new boards got big air. Riders had fun. They challenged themselves.

Snowboarders worked on bigger and better tricks. Some increased their speed. Some went to the **backcountry** instead. Backcountry means undeveloped places. They rode on uneven **terrain**, or land. They jumped over **obstacles**. Obstacles are objects on the path. They include rocks, trees, gaps, or cliffs.

EXTREME SNOWBOARDING:

Know the Lingo

Bail: to crash land

Big air: high, long jump

Fakie: riding backward

Gnarly: beyond rad, beyond extreme, perfection; dangerous

Goofy: left foot on tail, right foot on nose

Grommet: talented young snowboarder

Huck: fly wildly in the air on a board and then crash

Ollie: springing off the tail of the board and into the air

Rad: cool, radical

Run: going from top to bottom; includes obstacles and tricks

Shred: to snowboard hard and fast

Sick: really awesome

Sketching: nearly falling as you ride

Spin masters: snowboarders who pull off smooth turns in the air

Stick: a snowboard

Wipeout: falling or crashing

CHAPTER 3

There's a Style for Every Rider!

Extreme snowboarders want to be first. They invent new tricks. They work to be the fastest. They try new slopes no one else has gone down before. To do this, some travel to faraway places. There's a style to appeal to every rider.

FREESTYLE
SNOWBOARDING

Freestyle snowboarding is all about tricks. Snowboarders use obstacles and jumps to do tricks. They look for steep slopes. They use the halfpipe. The more air they get, the more extreme the tricks!

Riders do spins, flips, and grabs. They do **inverted aerials**. Inverted means upside down. Aerials are tricks in the air.

Riders combine moves. They create new tricks. Snowboarders get to name the tricks they create. Some examples include Spaghetti Air, Canadian Bacon, and Hot Garbage.

FREERIDE SNOWBOARDING

Freeride snowboarding is all about keeping it natural. With this style, snowboarders **carve** around and over natural features. To carve means to use the edge of the board to turn quickly. Riders board down **off-piste** trails. Off-piste means natural, unprepared slopes away from ski resorts.

Some riders look for tall mountains. They get to the top. Some use climbing gear. Some drop from helicopters. They search for places no one has snowboarded before. It's dangerous. The terrain is rough. It is extreme!

SÜDTIROL
VENEZIA GIULIA
www.turismofvg.it

ALPINE SNOWBOARDING

Alpine snowboarding is all about speed and skill. Snowboarders challenge themselves to go faster and faster down the slopes. They practice carving. They work hard to keep control of their boards.

BOARDERCROSS SNOWBOARDING

Boardercross is like motocross, but on snow. Motocross is when riders race motorcycles around dirt tracks. Boardercross is also a race. Athletes navigate around human-made obstacles on a course. These could include bumps or jumps.

JAMIE BARROW BEING TOWED BY A PLANE

SHRED IT!

When Extreme Is Too Extreme!

Jamie Barrow is a record-breaking snowboarder. But his journey to get there wasn't easy. In 2013, he was training for the Winter Olympics. He crashed and injured his back. Doctors told him he would probably not be able to walk again. But Barrow wouldn't accept that. He fought to get better. He started practicing to break records. Later that year, he broke the British snowboard speed record. Next, he set a record for fastest speed on a snowboard while propelled by electric jet engines! In 2022, he broke the record for fastest speed on a snowboard towed by a vehicle for the second time. He reached 131 miles (210.8 kilometers) per hour! Even outside of record breaking, Barrow loves a challenge. He was towed behind an airplane on his snowboard! The plane hit 78 miles (125.5 km) per hour on the runway. Barrow didn't let an injury stop him. And he's going to keep pushing it to the limit.

CHAPTER 4

Keep Shredding!

Mountain weather can be dangerous. Extreme snowboarders face strong winds. They deal with below-freezing temperatures. It may be cold. But they can still get sunburned. The sun reflects off the snow.

Riders wear winter gear to keep them warm. They need snow pants, coats, hats, and gloves. They also wear helmets and goggles for safety.

Xavier de Le Rue and **Lucas Debari** went to Antarctica. They were by themselves. They spent a month there. They climbed mountains for hours. They then snowboarded down. The slopes had never been ridden before. They learned as they explored. The terrain was rough. There were dangerous ice slabs. Mistakes could have been dangerous.

Weather can turn bad suddenly. Blizzards can hit. **Avalanches** are another risk. These huge snow slides often happen without warning. Extreme snowboarders respect the mountain. Anything can happen.

And anything did happen to Mark McMorris. He's a professional snowboarder. He wanted something different. So he went to the backcountry. He respected the mountain. But in 2017, he crashed. He ran into a tree. He had a broken jaw, left arm, and pelvis. He had broken ribs. He had a collapsed lung. He ruptured his spleen. He almost died. McMorris wasn't sure he'd be able to compete again.

McMorris didn't give up. He worked hard to get his strength back. He is back doing what he loves.

But his passion for snowboarding brought him back. Just 11 months later, he won a bronze medal at the Winter Olympics in Pyeongchang, South Korea. And he kept going. In 2021, he competed in the Natural Selection Tour and won the top spot in Jackson Hole, Wyoming. McMorris also won a silver medal in the 2025 X Games. Nothing keeps extreme snowboarders down.

SHRED IT!

Advice from the Field

Many extreme snowboarders take avalanche safety classes. It's best to rescue an avalanche victim within 15 minutes. They then have a 90 percent chance of survival. Anyone going to the backcountry should follow these tips.

+ If you head out to the backcountry, take a **beacon**. It is a device that gives off a signal. Rescuers can track the signal. They can find you in an emergency, even under snow.

+ If you're in an avalanche, do the following: Jump up the slope. Move to the side of the avalanche. Let go of gear except for safety gear. Hold on to something. Swim on your back toward the surface.

+ If you get buried, do the following: Hold one arm straight above your head. Spit to see which way is up. Dig an air pocket around your face. This gives you 30 minutes of breathing time. Stay calm to save air and energy.

GLOSSARY

aerials (AIR-ee-uhlz) tricks done in the air

avalanches (AV-uh-lanch-iz) large masses of snow moving quickly down a slope

backcountry (BAK-kuhn-tree) remote, natural areas away from ski resorts

beacon (BEE-kuhn) device that signals location

bindings (BIEND-ingz) straps that hold boots in place

carve (KARV) to use the edges of the board to turn quickly

halfpipe (HAF-piep) a U-shaped ramp

inverted (in-VER-tuhd) upside down

obstacles (AHB-stih-kuhlz) objects in the way of something

off-piste (ahf-PEEST) skiing or snowboarding down ungroomed trails or in the backcountry

prosthetic (prahs-THEH-tik) describes an artificial limb

rip (RIHP) to cut through

rivals (RIE-vuhlz) people who compete against each other

shred (SHRED) snowboarding hard and fast

terrain (tuh-RAYN) land

INDEX